UNPUBLISHED POEMS OF EMILY DICKINSON

Cocoon above! Cocoon below!
Stealthy Cocoon, why hide you so
What all the world suspect!
An hour, and gay on every tree
Your secret, perched in Ecstasy
Defies imprisonment!

An hour in Chrysalis to pass.
Then gay above receding grass
A Butterfly to go!
A moment to interrogate
Then wiser than a "Surrogate"
The Universe to know!

FACSIMILE OF A POEM BY EMILY DICKINSON
HERETOFORE UNPUBLISHED

(*See page 57*)

UNPUBLISHED POEMS OF EMILY DICKINSON

EDITED BY HER NIECE
MARTHA DICKINSON BIANCHI
AND ALFRED LEETE HAMPSON

LITTLE, BROWN, AND COMPANY

BOSTON 1935

Published November, 1935

PRINTED IN THE UNITED STATES OF AMERICA

This edition consists of
five hundred twenty-five numbered copies
of which five hundred are offered for sale.

This is copy 182

IN presenting these unpublished poems of Emily Dickinson — disclosed during the exhaustive examination of the Dickinson family papers made obligatory by the increasing posthumous fame of the poet — the editors wish to acknowledge their indebtedness to the instant response of the publishers and other recognized authorities, whose interest has been so large a factor in their publication at this time.

ONE

[3]

My triumph lasted till the drums
Had left the Dead alone,
And then I dropped my victory
And, chastened, stole along

To where the finished faces
Conclusion turned on me —
And then I hated glory
And wished myself were They!

What is to be — is best descried
When it has also been, —
Could Prospect taste of Retrospect
The tyrannies of men

Were tenderer, diviner
The Transitive toward.
A bayonet's contrition
Is nothing to the Dead!

MORE life went out, when He went,
Than ordinary breath,
Lit with a finer phosphor
Requiring in the quench

A power of renownéd cold —
The climate of the grave
A temperature just adequate
So anthracite to live.*

For some an ampler zero,
A frost more needle keen
Is necessary to reduce
The Ethiop within.

Others extinguish easier —
A gnat's minutest fan
Sufficient to obliterate
A tract of citizen.

*Appendix

5

So much of Heaven has gone from Earth
That there must be a Heaven,
If only to enclose the saints
To affidavit given.

The missionary to the mole
Must prove there is a sky!
Location doubtless he would urge —
But what excuse have I?

HE fought like those who've nought to lose;
Bestowed himself to balls
As one who for a further life
Had not a further use!

Invited Death with bold attempt;
But Death was coy of him
As other men were coy of Death!
To him, to live was doom.

His comrades shifted like the flakes
When gusts reverse the snow;
But he remained alive because
Of vehemence to die!

DID you ever stand in a cavern's mouth —
Widths out of the sun —
And look and shudder and block your breath
And deem to be alone
In such a place what horror,
How goblin it would be?
And fly as 'twere pursuing you? —
Then Loneliness looks so.

Did you ever look in a cannon's face
Between whose yellow eye
And yours the Judgement intervened,
The question of "to die"
Extemporizing in your ear
Distinct as satyrs' drums?
If you remember, and were saved,
It's liker *so*, it seems.

HE gave away his life —
To us gigantic sum ! —
A trifle in his own esteem,
But magnified by fame

Until it burst the hearts
That fancied they could hold,
When quick it slipped its limit
And on the Heavens unrolled.

'Tis ours to wince and weep —
And wonder — and decay
By blossom's gradual process ;
He chose maturity ! —

And ripening, as we sowed,
Just obviated bud ;
And when we turned to note the growth,
Broke perfect from the pod.

⟦ 9 ⟧

UNTO like story trouble has enticed me —
How kinsmen fell,
Brothers and sisters who preferred the glory
And their young will
Bent to the scaffold, or in dungeons chanted
Till God's full time —
When they let go the ignominy, smiling,
And shame went still.

Unto guessed crests my moaning fancy lures me,
Worn fair
By heads rejected in the lower country;
Of honors there
Such spirit makes perpetual mention
That I, grown cold,
Step martial at my crucifixion
As trumpets rolled.

Feet small as mine have marched in revolution
Firm to the drum;
Hands not so stout hoisted them in witness
When speech went numb.
Let me not shame their sublime deportments
Drilled bright —
Beckoning Etruscan invitation
Toward Light!

IF any sink, assure that this now standing
Failed like themselves and, conscious that it rose,
Grew by the fact — and not the understanding
How weakness passed or force arose.

Tell that the Worst is easy in a moment,
Dread — but the whizzing before the ball;
When the ball enters, enters silence —
Dying annuls the power to kill.

11

A TOOTH upon our peace
The peace cannot deface.
Then wherefore be the tooth?
To vitalize the Grace.

The Heaven hath a Hell
Itself to signalize,
And every sign before the place
Is gilt with sacrifice.

IF your Nerve deny you,
Go above your Nerve, —
You can lean against the Grave
If he fear to swerve.

That's a steady posture —
Never any bend
Held of those brass arms,
Best Giant made.

If your Soul see-saw,
Lift the Flesh door, —
The Poltroon wants oxygen —
Nothing more.

THE first Day's Night had come —
And, grateful that a thing
So terrible had been endured,
I told my Soul to sing.

She said her strings were snapt,
Her bow to atoms blown;
And so, to mend her, gave me work
Until another morn.

And then a Day as huge
As Yesterday in pairs
Unrolled its horror on my face —
Until it blocked my eyes.

SOMEHOW myself survived the night
And entered with the day;
That it be saved — the saved suffice
Without the formula.

Henceforth I take my living place
As one commuted, led
A candidate for morning chance —
But dated with the Dead.

[15]

To whom the mornings stand for nights,
What must the midnights be!

WE grow accustomed to the dark
When light is put away,
As when the neighbor hold the lamp
To witness her good-by

A moment we uncertain step
For newness of the night,
Then fit our vision to the dark
And meet the road, erect!

And so of larger darknesses —
Those evenings of the brain
When not a moon disclose a sign,
Or star come out, within.

The bravest grope a little
And sometimes hit a tree
Directly in the forehead, —
But, as they learn to see,

Either the darkness alters —
Or something in the sight
Adjusts itself to midnight —
And life steps almost straight.

THE lamp burns sure, within,
The serfs supply the oil, —
It matters not the busy wick
At her phosphoric toil!

The slave forgets to fill —
The lamp burns golden on,
Unconscious that the oil is out
As that the slave is gone!

[18]

A WEIGHT, with needles in the pounds
To push and pierce besides —
That if the flesh resist the heft,
The puncture coolly tries —

That not a pore be overlooked
Of all this compound frame;
As manifold for anguish
As spices be for name.

[19]

I AM afraid to own a body,
I am afraid to own a soul;
Profound, precarious property,
Possession not optional.

Double estate entailed at pleasure
Upon an unsuspecting heir;
Duke in a moment of deathlessness,
And God for a frontier.

20

DID our Best Moment last
'Twould supersede the Heaven.
A few, — and they by risk, — procure,
So this sort are not given

Except as stimulants
In cases of despair
Or stupor. The reserve
These heavenly moments are —

A grant of the Divine —
That certain as it comes,
Withdraws, and leaves the dazzled Soul
In her unfurnished room.

EXHILARATION is Within —
There can no Outer wine
So royally intoxicate
As that diviner brand

The Soul achieves, Herself,
To drink, or set away
For Visitor or Sacrament —
'Tis not of holiday.

To stimulate a May
Who hath the ample Rhine
Within his closet, best you can
Exhale in offering.

BOUND a trouble and lives will bear it, —
Circumscription enable woe;
Still to conjecture were no limit,
Who were sufficient to misery?

State it the ages to a cypher
And it will ache contented on —
Sing at its pain, like any workman,
Notching the fall of the even Sun.

[23]

I SAW no way, the Heavens were stitched,
I felt the columns close;
The Earth reversed her hemispheres,
I touched the Universe

And back it slid — and I alone,
A speck upon a ball,
Went out upon Circumference —
Beyond the dip of bell!

WHAT twigs we held by! Oh the view
When, life's swift river striven through,
We pause before another plunge
To take momentum! As the fringe
Upon a former garment shows
The garment cast, our props disclose
So scant, so eminently small,
Of might to help so pitiful,
To sink if we had labored fond
The diligence were not more blind.

How scant by everlasting light
The discs that satisfied our sight!
How dimmer than a Saturn's bar
The things esteemed for things that are!

MUST be a woe,
A loss or so
To bend the eye
Best beauty's way.

But once aslant,
It gains delight
As classified
As stalactite.

A common bliss
Were had for less,
The price — is
Even as the Grace.

Our Lord thought no
Extravagance
To pay — a Cross!

THE Martyr Poets did not tell,
But wrought their pang in syllable, —
That when their mortal fame be numb
Their mortal fate encourage some.

The Martyr Painters never spoke,
Bequeathing rather to their work, —
That when their conscious fingers cease
Some seek in Art the Art of Peace.

FOR this accepted Breath,
Through it compete with Death,
The fellow cannot touch this Crown!
By it my title take,
Ah! what a royal sake
To my necessity stooped down!

No wilderness can be
Where this attendeth me;
No desert noon,
No fear of frost to come
Haunt the perennial bloom,
But certain June!

Get Gabriel to tell
The royal syllable;
Get Saints with new unsteady tongue
To say what trance below
Most like their glory show —
Fittest the Crown!

The second stanza (with a slight variant) was sent to Samuel Bowles about 1864. See "The Life and Letters of Emily Dickinson", Martha Dickinson Bianchi, Houghton Mifflin; p. 254.

TWO

31

TIME feels so vast
That were it not for an Eternity,
I fear me this Circumference
Engross my Finity

To His exclusion,
Who prepares by rudiments of size
For the stupendous volume
Of his Diameters.

I SHALL keep singing! Birds will pass me
On their way to yellower climes;
Each with a robin's expectation, —
I with my redbreast and my rhymes.

Late — when I take my place in Summer,
But I shall sing a fuller tune;
Vespers are sweeter than Matins, Signor, —
Morning, only the seed of Noon.

[33]

IT'S thoughts and just one heart
And old sunshine about
Make frugal one's content —
And two or three for company
Upon a holiday
Crowded as Sacrament.

Books — when the unit
Spare the tenant long eno' —
A picture, if it care,
Itself a gallery too rare
For needing more;
Flowers to keep the eyes
From going awkward when it snows;
A bird, if they prefer,
Though Winter fire sing clear as plover
To our ear;
A landscape, not so great
To suffocate the eye;
A hill perhaps,
Perhaps the profile of a mill
Turned by the wind —
Though such are luxuries.

It's thoughts and just one heart
And Heaven about —
At least a counterfeit
We would not have correct —
And Immortality can be
Almost —
Not quite — content.

THEY shut me up in prose —
As when, a little girl,
They put me in the closet
Because they liked me "still."

"Still!" Could themselves have peeped
And seen my brain go round,
They might as wise have lodged a bird
For treason in the pound!

Himself has but to will,
And, easy as a star,
Look down upon captivity
And laugh. Nor more have I!

I'M saying every day
"If I should be a Queen tomorrow
I'd do this way," —
And so I deck a little
If it be I wake a Bourbon
None on me bend supercilious
With "This was she
Begged in the market place
Yesterday."
Court is a stately place
I've heard men say,
So I loop my apron against the majesty
With bright pins of buttercup —
That not too plain
Rank overtake me —
And perch my tongue
On twigs of singing, rather high,
But this might be my brief term
To qualify, —
Put from my simple speech
All plain word,
Take other accents
As such I heard —
Though but for the cricket, just,
And but for the bee
Not in all the meadow
One accost me.
Better be ready
Than did next morn
Meet me in Arragon
My old gown on,

And the surprised air
Rustics wear
Summoned unexpectedly
To Exeter.

NEVER for society
One shall seek in vain
Who his own acquaintance
Cultivate. Of men
Wiser ear may weary,
But the man within
Never knew satiety,
Better entertain
Than could border ballad
Or Biscayan hymn;
Neither introduction
Need you unto him.

I'VE heard an organ talk sometimes
In a cathedral aisle
And understood no word it said,
Yet held my breath the while

And risen up and gone away
A more Bernardine girl,
Yet knew not what was done to me
In that old hallowed aisle.

I THINK I was enchanted
When first, a little girl,
I read that Foreign Lady [1] —
The dark felt beautiful!

And whether it was noon at night,
Or only heaven at noon,
For very lunacy of light
I had not power to tell.

The bees became as butterflies,
The butterflies as moons
Lit up the low inferior grass;
And just the common tunes

That Nature murmured to herself,
To keep herself in cheer,
I took for Giants practising
Titanic opera.

The days to mighty metres stept,
The homeliest adorned
As if unto a Jubilee
'Twere suddenly confirmed.

I could not have defined the change —
Conversion of the mind,
Like sanctifying in the Soul,
Is witnessed, not explained.

[1] Elizabeth Barrett Browning

'Twas a divine insanity.
The sorrow to be sane
Should I again experience,
'Tis antidote to turn

To tomes of solid witchcraft.
Magicians be asleep,
But magic hath an element
Like Deity to keep!

A MIEN to move a queen —
Half child, half heroine —
An Orleans in the eye
That puts its manner by
For humbler company
When none are near —
Even a tear
Its frequent visitor.
A bonnet like a duke —
And yet a wren's peruke
Were not so shy
Of goer-by —
And hands so slight
They would elate a sprite
With merriment.
A voice that alters — low —
And on the ear can go
Like set of snow,
Or shift supreme
As tone of realm
On subject's diadem —
Too small to fear,
Too distant to endear, —
And so men compromise
And just revere.

THE Winters are so short
I'm hardly justified
In sending all the birds away,
And moving into pod

Myself, — for, scarcely settled,
The phoebes have begun,
And then it's time to strike my tent,
And open house, again.

It's mostly interruptions,
My Summer is despoiled
Because there was a Winter once —
And all the cattle starved.

And so there was a Deluge
And swept the World away, —
But Ararat's a legend now —
And no one credits Noah!

MY first well day, since many ill,
I asked to go abroad
And take the sunshine in my hands
And see the things in pod —

A'blossom just when I went in
To take my chance with Pain,
Uncertain if Myself — or He —
Should prove the strongest One.

The Summer deepened while we strove:
She put some flowers away
And redder cheeked ones in their stead —
A fond elusive way

To cheat herself it seemed she tried,
As if before a child
To fade tomorrow, rainbows held
The sepulchre could hide.

She dealt a fashion to the nut,
She tied the hoods to seeds,
She dropped bright scraps of tint about
And left Brazilian threads

On every shoulder that she met —
Then both her hands of haze
Put up to hide her panting grace
From our unfitted eyes.

[44]

My loss by sickness — was it loss?
Or that ethereal gain
One earns by measuring the Grave —
Then — measuring the Sun!

THE day undressed herself —
Her garter was of gold,
Her petticoat of purple,
Her dimities as old

Precisely as the world!
And yet the newest star
Unrolled upon the firmament
Be wrinkled much as her.

Too near to God to pray,
Too near to Heaven to fear,
The Lady of the Occident
Retired without a care.

Her candle so expire
The flickering be seen
On ball of mast in foreign port,
On Bosphorus and dome.

A SLASH of Blue, a sweep of Gray!
Some Scarlet patches on the way
Compose an evening sky!
A little Purple slipped between,
Some Ruby trousers hurried on,
A wave of Gold, and Bank of Day, —
This just makes out the morning sky!

A VISITOR in March —
Who influences flowers
Till they are orderly as busts
And elegant as glass, —

Who visits in the night —
And just before the sun,
Concludes his glistening interview,
Caresses — and is gone.

But whom his fingers touched —
And where his feet have run —
And whatsoever mouth he kissed —
Is as it had not been!

(Jack Frost)

HAVE any, like myself,
Investigating March,
New houses on the hills descried
And possibly a church

That were *not*, we are sure,
As lately as the snow,
And *are* today, — if we exist, —
Though how may this be so?

Have any, like myself,
Conjectured who may be
The occupants of these abodes
So easy to the sky

'Twould seem that God should be
The nearest Neighbor to,
And Heaven a convenient grace
For show, or company?

Have any, like myself,
Preserved the charm secure
By shunning carefully the place
All seasons of the year

Excepting March? — 'Tis then
My villages be seen,
And possibly a steeple,
Not afterward — by men.

THE birds reported from the South
A news express to me;
A spicy charge, my little posts,
But I am deaf today.

The flowers appealed — a timid throng —
I re-enforced the door;
"Go, Blossom, to the bees," I said,
"And trouble me no more!"

The summer grace for notice strove,
Remote her best array;
The heart to stimulate the eye
Refused too utterly.

At length a mourner like myself,
She drew away austere
Her frosts to ponder, — then it was
I recollected her.

She suffered me, for I had mourned, —
I offered her no word;
My witness was the black I bore,
Her witness was the Dead.

Thence forward we together dwelt;
She never questioned me,
Nor I herself, — our compact
A wordless sympathy.

AN ignorance a sunset
Confer upon the eye
Of territory, color,
Circumference, decay.

Its amber revelation
Exhilarate, debase, —
Omnipotence' inspection
Of our inferior face.

And when the solemn features
Confirm, in victory,
We start, as if detected
In Immortality.

THE trees, like tassels, hit and swung;
There seemed to rise a tune
From miniature creatures
Accompanying the Sun,

The Psalteries of Summer,
Enamouring the ear
They never yet did satisfy —
Remotest when most near.

The Sun shone whole at intervals,
Then half, — then utter hid,
As if himself were optional
And had estates of clouds

Sufficient to enfold him
Eternally from view,
Except it were a whim of his
To let the orchards grow.

A bird sat careless on the fence;
One gossiped in the lane
On silver matters, charmed a snake
Just winding round a stone.

Bright flowers slit a calyx,
Or soared upon a stem
Like hindered flags, sweet hoisted,
With spices in the hem.

'Twas more I cannot mention.
How mean, to those that see,
Van Dyke's delineation
Of Nature's Summer day!

I KNOW where wells grow — droughtless wells —
Deep dug for Summer days,
Where mosses go no more away,
And pebble safely plays.

They're made of fathoms and a belt,
A belt of jagged stone
Inlaid with emerald half way down,
And diamonds jumbled on.

They have no bucket, — were I rich
A bucket I would buy;
I'm often thirsty, but my lips
Are so high up, you see.

I read in an old-fashioned Book
That people "thirst no more";
The wells have buckets to them, there, —
It must mean that, I'm sure.

Shall we remember parching, then?
Those Waters sound so grand!
I think a little well like mine
Dearer to understand.

WHEN diamonds are a legend,
And diadems a tale,
I brooch and earrings for myself
Do sow, and raise for sale.

And though I'm scarce accounted,
My art a Summer day
Had patrons; once it was a Queen,
And once a Butterfly!

"ANSWER, July! —
Where is the Bee —
Where is the Blush —
Where is the Hay?"

"Ah," said July,
"Where is the Seed —
Where is the Bud —
Where is the May? —
Answer Thee me!"

"Nay," said the May,
"Show me the Snow —
Show me the Bells —
Show me the Jay!"

Quibbled the Jay,
"Where be the Maize —
Where be the Haze —
Where be the Burr?"
"Here!" — said the Year.

HE parts himself like leaves,
And then he closes up, —
Then stands upon the bonnet
Of any Buttercup.

And then he runs against
And oversets a Rose,
And then does nothing, —
Then away upon a jiff he goes,

And dangling like a mote
Suspended in the Noon,
Uncertain to return Below
Or settle in the Moon.

What came of him at night,
The privilege to say
Be limited by ignorance
What came of him that day.

The Frost obtain the world,
In cabinets be shown
A Sepulchre of quaintest floss,
An Abbey — a Cocoon.

COCOON above! Cocoon below!
Stealthy Cocoon, why hid you so
What all the world suspect?
An hour, and gay on every tree
Your secret perched in ecstasy
Defies imprisonment!

An hour in Chrysalis to pass,
Then gay above receding grass
A Butterfly to go!
A moment to interrogate,
Then wiser than a "Surrogate"
The universe to know!

SOME such butterfly be seen
On Brazilian Pampas
Just at noon — no later,
Then sweet license closes.

Some such spice express and pass
Subject to your plucking —
As the stars you knew last night,
Foreigners, this morning.

[59]

MY garden, like the beach,
Denotes there be a sea that's Summer —
Such as these the pearls
She fetches such as me.

(Sent with flowers)

THEMSELVES are all I have —
Myself a freckled be.
I thought you'd choose a velvet cheek
Or one of ivory.
Would you instead of me?

(Sent with flowers)

THE Grace myself might not obtain
Confer upon my flower;
Refracted but a countenance,
For I inhabit her.

[62]

BUT little carmine hath her face,
Of emerald scant, her gown;
Her beauty is the love she doth,
Itself enable mine!

(With a flower)

THIS bauble was preferred by bees —
By butterflies desired —
At heavenly hopeless distance
Of bird was justified —
Did Noon embellish in herself —
Was Summer to a score
Who only knew of Universe
It had created her.

THE Flower must not blame the Bee
That seeketh his felicity
Too often at her door, —
But teach the footman from Vevay
Mistress is "not at home" to say
To people, any more!

SHE hideth her the last,
And is the first to rise;
Her night doth hardly recompense
The closing of her eyes.

She doth her purple work,
And putteth her away
In low apartments in the sod
As worthily as we.

To imitate her life
As possible would be
As brew from our obtuser mints
The julep of the Bee!

THE Himalah was known to stoop
Unto the daisy low,
Transported with compassion
That such a doll should grow,
When, tent by tent, her universe
Hung out its flags of snow.

IN Ebon Box, when years have flown,
To reverently peer,
Wiping away the velvet dust
Summers have sprinkled there!

To hold a letter to the light —
Grown tawny now with time —
To con the faded syllables
That quickened us like wine!

Perhaps a flower's shrivelled cheek
Among its stores to find,
Plucked far away some morning
By gallant, mouldering hand!

A curl, perhaps, from foreheads
Our Constancy forget;
Perhaps an antique trinket
In vanished fashions set!

And then to lay them quiet back
And go about its care,
As if the little Ebon Box
Were none of our affair!

I PLAY at riches to appease
The clamoring for gold;
It kept me from a thief, I think,
For often, over bold

With want and opportunity,
I might have done a sin
And been myself that distant thing —
An independent man!

But often as my lot displays
Too hungry to be borne,
I deem myself what I would be, —
And so much comforting

My poverty and I derive,
We question if the man
Who own, esteem the opulence
As we, who never can.

Should ever these exploring hands
Chance sovereign on a mine,
Or in the long uneven term
To win become their turn,

How fitter they will be for want
Enlightening so well!
I know not which — desire or grant —
Be wholly beautiful!

THE Outer from the Inner
Derives its magnitude;
'Tis duke or dwarf according
As is the central mood

The fine unvarying axis
That regulates the wheel,
Though spokes spin more conspicuous
And fling a dust the while.

The Inner paints the Outer;
The brush without the hand
Its picture publishes precise
As is the inner brand

On fine arterial canvas —
A cheek, perchance a brow.
The stars' whole secret in the lake
Eyes were not meant to know.

SIZE circumscribes, it has no room
For petty furniture;
The Giant tolerates no Gnat
For ease of Gianture —

Repudiates it, all the more,
Because intrinsic size
Ignores the possibility
Of Calumnies or Flies.

MYSELF was formed a carpenter.
An unpretending time
My plans and I together wrought
Before a builder came

To measure our attainments —
Had we the Art of Boards
Sufficiently developed
He'd hire us at halves.

My tools took human faces,
The bench where we had toiled
Against the man persuaded.
"We temples build," I said.

"HAD I not This — or This," I said,
  Appealing to myself
In moment of prosperity,
  "Inadequate were life."

"Thou hast not Me — or Me!" it said
  In moment of reverse,
"And yet thou art industrious —
  No need hadst thou of Us."

"My need was all I had," I said.
  The need did not reduce;
Because the food exterminate
  The hunger does not cease,

But diligence is sharper
  Proportioned to the chance;
To feed upon the retrograde
  Enfeebles the advance.

REMOVED from accident of loss
By accident of gain
Befalling not my simple days,
Myself had just to earn.

Of riches as unconscious
As is the brown Malay
Of pearls in Eastern waters
Marked his. What holiday

Would stir his slow conception
Had he the power to dream
That but the dower's fraction
Awaited even — him!

TRUST in the Unexpected!
By this was William Kidd
Persuaded of the buried gold,
As one had testified.

Through this the old philosopher
His Talismanic Stone
Discerned, — still withholden
To effort undivine.

'Twas this allured Columbus
When Genoa withdrew
Before an apparition
Baptized America.

The same afflicted Thomas
When Deity assured
'Twas better — the perceiving *not*,
Provided it believed!

UNFULFILLED to observation,
Incomplete to eye —
But to Faith a revelation
In locality —
Unto us the suns extinguish.
To our opposite
New horizons they replenish,
Fronting us with night.

WE dream, — it is good we are dreaming,
It would hurt us were we awake;
But since it is playing kill us,
And we are playing shriek,

What harm? Men die externally,
It is a truth of Blood, —
But we are dying in Drama,
And Drama is never dead.

Cautions we give each other,
And seldom open the eyes
Lest the phantasm prove the mistake just,
And the livid surprise

Cool us to shafts of granite,
With just an age and name
And perhaps a Latin inscription.
It's prudenter to dream!

DREAMS are well, but waking's better
  If one wakes at morn!
If one wake at midnight better
  Dreaming of the dawn.

Sweeter the surmising robins
  Never gladdened tree,
Than a solid dawn confronting,
  Leading to no day.

To put this world down like a bundle
And walk away
Requires energy — possibly agony;
'Tis the scarlet Way

Trodden with straight renunciation
By the Son of God;
Later, his faint confederates
Justify the Road.

Flavors of that old Crucifixion,
Filaments of bloom
Pontius Pilate sowed, — strong clusters
From Barrabas' tomb.

Sacraments Saints partook before us,
Patent — every drop —
With the Brand of the Gentile Drinker
Who indorsed the Cup.

79

I SOMETIMES drop it, for a quick,
The thought to be alive —
Anonymous delight to know
And madder to conceive

Consoles a woe so monstrous,
That did it tear all day
Without an instant's respite —
'Twould look too far to die.

Delirium diverts the wretch
For whom the scaffold neighs;
The hammock's motion calls the heads
So close on Paradise.

A reef crawled easy from the sea
Eats off the brittle line;
The sailor doesn't know the stroke,
Until he's past the pain.

A PLATED life diversified
With gold and silver pain
To prove the presence of the ore
In particles! 'Tis when
A nature struggle, it exist.
A power will proclaim,
Although annihilation pile
Whole chaoses on him!

THREE

YOU'LL know it as you know 'tis Noon —
By Glory! As you do the Sun —
By Glory! As you will in Heaven
Know God the Father and the Son!

By intuition mightiest things
Assert themselves, and not by terms.
"I'm Midnight," need the Midnight say?
"I'm Sunrise," need the Majesty?

Omnipotence had not a tongue:
His lisp is Lightning and the Sun,
His conversation with the Sea.
"How shall you know?" Consult your eye!

A TRANSPORT one cannot contain
May yet a transport be,
Though God forbid it lift the lid
Unto its ecstasy!

A diagram of rapture
A sixpence at a show!
With Seraphim in cages
The Universe would go!

I THINK to live may be a bliss,
To those who dare to try,
Beyond my limit to conceive,
My lips to testify.

I think the heart I former wore
Could widen — till to me
The other, like the little bank
Appear unto the Sea.

I think the days could every one
In ordination stand,
And majesty be easier
Than an inferior kind.

No numb alarm lest difference come,
No goblin on the bloom,
No start in apprehension's ear,
No bankruptcy, no doom, —

But certainties of sun,
Mid-summer in the mind,
A steadfast south upon the soul,
Her polar time behind.

The vision, pondered long,
So plausible becomes
That I esteem the fiction real —
The real, fictitious seems.

[86]

How beautiful the dream!
What plenty it would be
Had all my life but been mistake
Just rectified by Thee!

THE Heaven vest for each
In that small Deity
It craved the grace to worship
Some bashful Summer's day,

Half shrinking from the glory
It importuned to see,
Till these faint tabernacles drop
In full eternity.

How imminent the venture —
As one should sue a star
For his mean sake to leave the row
And entertain despair!

A clemency so common
We almost cease to fear,
Enabling the minutest
And furthest to adore!

YOU know that portrait in the moon,
So tell me who 'tis like —
The very brow, the stooping eyes
A-fog for — say, whose sake?

The very pattern of the cheek,
It varies in the chin, —
But Ishmael, since *we* met 'tis long —
And fashions intervene.

When morn's at full 'tis Thou, I say,
My lips just hold the name, —
When crescent — Thou art worn I note,
But there the golden same.

And when some night bold slashing clouds
Cut Thee away from me,
That's easier than the other film
That glazes holiday.

MANY a phrase has the English language, —
I have heard but one
Low as the laughter of the cricket,
Loud as the thunder's tongue;

Murmuring like old Caspian choirs
When the tide's a'lull,
Saying itself in new inflection
Like a whippoorwill;

Breaking in bright orthography
On my simple sleep;
Thundering its perspective
Till I stir and weep —

Not for the sorrow done me,
But for the push of joy;
Say it again — Saxon!
Hush — only to me!

PROMISE this, when you be dying
Some shall summon me;
Mine belong your latest sighing,
Mine to belt your eye —

Not with coins, though they be minted
From an Emperor's hand;
Be my lips the only buckle
Your low eyes demand.

Mine to stay, when all have wandered,
To devise once more
If the life be too surrendered
Life of mine restore.

Poured like this, my whole libation,
Just that you should see
Bliss of Death Life's bliss surpass
In more resembling you.

Mine to guard your narrow precinct,
To entice the sun
Longest on your south to linger;
Regal dews of morn

To demand, in your low favor,
Lest the jealous grass
Greener lean, or fonder cluster
Round some other face.

Mine to supplicate Madonna,
If Madonna be
Could regard so scarce a creature, —
Christ omitted me.

Just to follow your dear features,
Ne'er so far behind,
For my Heaven, of all Her glories
Worthiest to have gained.

THAT first day when you praised me, Sweet,
And said that I was strong
And could be mighty, if I liked, —
That day, the days among,

Glows central, like a Jewel
Between diverging golds:
The minor one that gleamed behind,
And Master of the Worlds!

NOT probable — the merest chance –
A smile too few — a word too much —
And far from Heaven as the rest
The soul so close on Paradise.

What if the bird from journey far,
Confused by sweets, as mortals are,
Forget the secret of his wing
And perish — but a bough between?
Oh groping feet — oh phantom Queen!

AH Moon and Star!
You are very far —
But were no one further than you,
Do you think I'd stop for a Firmament —
Or a Cubit — or so?

I could borrow a bonnet of the lark,
And a chamois' silver boot,
And a stirrup of an antelope,
And be with you — Tonight!

But, Moon and Star,
Though you're very far,
There is One — further than you, —
He is more than Firmament from me,
So I can never go!

I COULD suffice for Him, I knew,
He could suffice for me;
Yet hesitating Fractions, Both
Surveyed Infinity.

"Would I be whole?" He sudden broached.
My syllable rebelled;
'Twas face to face with Nature forced,
'Twas face to face with God.

Withdrew the Sun to other Wests,
Withdrew the furthest Star
Before Decision stooped to speech,
And then be audibler

The answer of the Sea unto
The motion of the Moon,
Herself adjust her tides unto, —
Could I do else with mine?

THE day that I was crowned
Was like the other days,
Until the Coronation came —
And then, 'twas otherwise!

As carbon in the coal
And carbon in the gem
Are one, and yet — the former
Were dull for diadem.

I rose, and all was plain, —
But when the day declined,
Myself and it in majesty
Were equally adorned.

The Grace that I was chose,
To me, surpassed the Crown
That was the Witness for the Grace, —
'Twas even that 'twas mine!

WITHOUT this there is nought;
All other riches be
As is the twitter of the bird
Heard opposite the sea.

I could not care to gain
A lesser than the whole;
For did not this include themselves,
As seams include the ball?

Or wished a way might be
My heart to subdivide,
'Twould magnify the gratitude
And not reduce the gold.

IT would never be common more, I said,
Difference had begun;
Many a bitterness had been,
But that old sort was done.

Or if it sometimes showed, as 'twill
Upon the downiest morn,
Such bliss had I for all the years
'Twould give an easier pain.

I'd so much joy I told it red
Upon my simple cheek;
I felt it publish in my eye,
'Twas needless any speak.

I walked as wings of body bore,
The feet I former used
Unnecessary now to me
As boots would be to birds.

I put my pleasure all abroad,
I dealt a word of gold
For every creature that I met,
And dowered all the world.

When suddenly my riches shrank!
A goblin drank my dew —
My palaces dropped tenantless —
Myself was beggared too.

[99]

I clutched at sands — I groped at shapes —
I touched the tops of films,
I felt the wilderness roll back
Along my golden lines.

The sack cloth hangs upon the nail,
The frock I used to wear,
But where my moment of brocade —
My drop of India?

THEY put us far apart,
As separate as Sea
And her unsown peninsula, —
We signified "These see."

They took away our eyes,
They thwarted us with guns, —
"I see Thee" each responded straight,
Through telegraphic signs.

With dungeons they devised,
But through their thickest skill
And their opaquest adamant
Our Souls saw just as well.

They summoned us to die.
With sweet alacrity
We stood upon our stapled feet
Condemned, but first to see!

Permission to recant,
Permission to forget, —
We turned our backs upon the Sun
For perjury of that!

Not either noticed Death,
Of Paradise aware, —
Each Other's face was all the Disc
Each Other's setting saw.

TO make one's toilette, after Death
Has made the toilette cool
To only taste we care to please,
Is difficult; and still —

That's easier than braid the hair
And make the bodice gay,
When eyes that fondled it are wrenched
By Decalogues away.

IT might have been lonelier
Without the loneliness;
I'm so accustomed to my fate
Perhaps the other — peace —

Would interrupt the dark,
And crowd the little room —
Too scant, by cubits, to contain
The Sacrament of Him.

I am not used to hope:
It might intrude upon —
Its sweet parade blaspheme the place
Ordained to suffering.

It might be easier
To fail with land in sight
Than gain my blue peninsula —
To perish — of delight.

FORGET? The lady with the amulet
Forget she wore it at her heart
Because she breathed against?
Was treason 'twixt?

Deny? Did rose her bee
For privilege of play
Or will of butterfly
Or opportunity, her Lord away?

The lady with the amulet will fade;
The bee in mausoleum laid
Discard his bride;
But longer than the little rill

That cooled the forehead of the hill
While other went the sea to fill,
And other went to turn the mill,
I'll do thy will.

I WOULD die to know — 'tis a trifling knowledge —
News-boys salute the door, carts joggle by,
Morning's bold face stares in the window, —
Were but mine the charter of the least fly!

Houses hunch the house with their brick shoulders,
Coals from a rolling load rattle — how near
To the very square his foot is passing —
Possibly this moment! — while I dream here.

LET us play yesterday —
I the girl at school,
You and Eternity
The untold tale.

Easing my famine
At your lexicon,
Logarithm had I for drink —
'Twas a dry wine.

Somewhat different must be
Dreams tint the sleep,
Cunning reds of morning
Make the blind leap.

Still at the egg-life,
Chafing the shell,
When you troubled the ellipse —
And the bird fell.

Manacles be dim, they say,
To the new free, —
Liberty commoner
Never could to me.

'Twas my last gratitude
When I slept at night,
'Twas the first miracle
Let in with the light.

Can the lark resume the shell
Easier for the sky?
Wouldn't bonds hurt more
Than yesterday?

Wouldn't dungeons sorer grate
On the man — free —
Just long enough to taste —
Then doomed new?

God of the manacle
As of the free,
Take not my liberty
Away from me!

A SINGLE screen of flesh
Is all that pins the soul
That stands for Deity to mine,
Upon my side the vale.

Once witnessed of the gauze,
Its name is put away
As far from mine as if no plight
Had printed yesterday

In tender, solemn alphabet.
My eyes just turned to see —
When it was smuggled by my sight
Into Eternity.

More hands to hold! — these are but two —
One more new-mailéd nerve
Just granted for the peril's sake —
Some striding giant love

So greater than the gods can show
They shrink before the clay,
That not for all their heaven can boast
Will let its keepsake go.

IF he dissolve — then there is nothing more,
Eclipse at midnight — it was dark before!

Sunset at Easter — blindness on the dawn,
Faint Star of Bethlehem gone down!

I CROSS till I am weary
A mountain in my mind,
More mountains, then a sea, more seas,
And then a desert find.

And my horizon blocks
With steady drifting grains,
Of unconjectured quantity —
As Asiatic rains.

Nor this defeat my pace —
It hinder from the West
But as an enemy's salute
One hurrying to rest.

What merit had the goal
Except there intervene
Faint doubt, and far competitor
To jeopardize the gain?

At last the grace in sight,
I shout unto my feet —
Offer them the half of Heaven
The instant that We meet.

They strive — and yet delay;
They perish. Do we die —
Or is this Death's experiment
Reversed in Victory?

WE prove it now, whoever doubt,
We stop to prove it, now.
Make haste the scruple! Death be scant
For opportunity!

The River reaches to my feet,
And yet my heart be dry!
Oh Lover, Life could not convince,
Might Death enable Thee!

The River reaches to my breast, —
Still, still my hands above
Proclaim with their remaining might —
Dost recognize the Love?

The River reaches to my mouth, —
Remember, when the Sea
Swept by my searching eyes the last —
Themselves were quick with Thee!

FOUR

SEXTON! my Master's sleeping here,
Pray lead me to his bed!
I came to build the Bird's nest
And sow the early seed,

That when the snow creeps slowly
From off his Chamber door,
Daisies point the way there,
And the Troubadour.

IF I could bribe them by a Rose
I'd bring them every flower that grows
From Amherst to Cashmere!
I would not stop for night or storm,
Or frost or death or Anyone,
My business were so dear!

If they would linger for a Bird,
My tambourine were soonest heard
Among the April woods!
Unwearied all the summer long
Only to break in wilder song
When winter shook the boughs!

What if they hear me! Who shall say
That such an importunity
May not at last avail?
That weary of this Beggar's face
They may not finally say Yes,
To drive me from the Hall?

TOO little way the house must lie
From every human heart
That holds in undisputed lease
A white inhabitant.

For narrow is the right between,
Too imminent the chance;
Each consciousness must emigrate
And lose its neighbor once.

'TIS well, the looking back on grief,
To re-endure a day
We thought the mighty funeral
Of all conceived by joy;

To recollect how busy grass
Did meddle, one by one,
Till all the grief with Summer waved —
And none could see the stone.

And though the woe you have today
Be larger, as the sea
Exceeds its unremembered drop —
They prove one chemistry.

THE months have end, the years a knot
No power can untie,
To stretch a little further
A skein of misery.

The Earth lays back these tired lives
In her mysterious drawers
Too tenderly that any doubt
An ultimate repose;

The manner of the children
Who weary of the day,
Themselves the noisy plaything
They cannot put away.

BEREAVEMENT in their death to feel
Whom we have never seen,
A vital kinsmanship impart
Our soul and theirs, between.

For stranger — strangers do not mourn —
There be Immortal friends
Whom Death see first. 'Tis news of this
That paralyze ourselves.

Who, vital only to our thought,
Such presence bear away
In dying, 'tis as if our souls
Absconded suddenly.

[119]

'TWAS awkward, but it fitted me,
An ancient-fashioned heart;
Its only love its steadfastness,
In change unerudite.

It only swerved as do the suns
For merit of return,
Or birds confirmed perpetual
By alternating zone.

I only have it not tonight
In its established place
For technicality of Death —
Omitted in the lease.

BECAUSE 'twas riches I could own,
Myself had earned it me,
I knew the dollars by their names,
It feels like poverty

An earldom out of sight to hold,
An income in the air.
Possession has a sweeter chink
Unto a miser's ear.

[121]

TAKE your Heaven further on —
This to Heaven divine has gone.
Had you earlier blundered in
Possibly e'en you had seen
An Eternity put on.
Now to ring a door beyond
Is the utmost of your hand.
To the Skies apologize —
Nearer to your courtesies
Than this sufferer polite
Dressed to meet you, see — in white!

122

IT knew no medicine —
It was not sickness, then,
Nor any need of surgery —
And therefore, 'twas not pain.

It moved away the cheeks
A dimple at a time,
And left the profile plainer;
And in the stead of bloom

It left the little tint
That never had a name —
You've seen it on a cast's face;
Was Paradise to blame

If, her sweet door ajar,
Temerity drew near
And sickened ever afterward
For whatsoe'er it saw?

HER smile was shaped like other smiles:
The dimples ran along —
And still it hurt you, as some bird
Did hoist herself to sing —

Then recollect a ball she got,
And hold upon the twig,
Convulsive, while the music cracked —
Like beads among the bog.

But this one wears a merriment
So patient, like a pain
Fresh gilded to elude the eyes
Unqualified to scan.

No notice gave she but a change, —
No message but a sigh —
For whom — the time did not suffice
That she should specify.

She was not warm, though Summer shone,
Nor scrupulous of cold,
Though rime by rime the steady Frost
Upon her bosom piled.

Of shrinking ways, forebore her fright
Though all the village looked,
But held her gravity aloft
And met the gaze direct.

Then when adjusted like a seed
In careful fitted ground
Unto the Everlasting Spring,
And hindered but a mound

Her warm return, if so she chose,
And we, imploring, drew, —
Removed our invitation by
As some she never knew.

THESE saw vision, latch them softly;
These held dimples, smooth them slow;
This addressed departing accents —
Quick, sweet mouth, to miss them so.

This we stroked, unnumbered satin;
Those we held among our own —
Fingers of the slim Aurora
Not so arrogant this noon.

These adjust that ran to meet us,
Pearl for stocking — pearl for shoe;
Paradise the only palace
Fit for her reception — now.

TO die takes just a little while —
They say it doesn't hurt;
It's only fainter by degrees,
And then — it's out of sight.

A darker ribbon for a day,
A crape upon the hat;
And then the pretty sunshine comes
And helps us to forget

The absent, mystic Creature,
That but for love of us,
Had gone to sleep that soundest time
Without the weariness.

HER sweet turn to leave the homestead
Came the darker way;
Carriages, be sure, and guests too, —
But for holiday

'Twas more pitiful endeavour
Than did swelling sea
O'er the curls attempt to caper
It had cast away.

Never bride had such assembling;
Never kinsman kneeled
To salute so fair a forehead,
Garlanded indeed.

Fitter feet of Her before us,
Than whatever brow
Art of snow or trick of lily
Ever could endow.

Of her father whoso claim Her,
He shall seek as high
As the palm that serve the desert
To obtain the sky.

He must pass the crystal angle
That obscure Her face;
He must have achieved in person
Equal Paradise.

Distance be Her only motion;
If 'tis Nay — or Yes —
Acquiescence or demurrer —
Whosoever guess.

SHE lay as if at play
Her life had leaped away
Intending to return —
But not so soon.

Her merry arms half dropt
As if for lull of sport
An instant had forgot
The trick to start.

Her dancing eyes ajar
As if their owner were
Still sparkling through
For fun at you.

Her morning at the door,
Devising, I am sure,
To force her sleep —
So light, so deep.

SHE bore it till the simple veins
Traced azure on her hand,
Till pleading, round her quiet eye,
The purple crayons stand;

Till daffodils had come and gone,
I cannot tell the sum,
And then she ceased to bear it —
And with the Saints sat down.

No more her patient figure
At twilight soft to meet,
No more the timid bonnet
Upon the village street,

But crowns instead and courtiers, —
And in the midst so fair
Whose but her shy immortal face
Of whom we're whispering here!

THIS heart that broke so long —
These feet that never flagged —
This faith that watched for Star in vain
Give gently to the Dead.

Hound cannot overtake the hare
That fluttered panting here —
Nor any school-boy rob the nest
Tenderness builded there.

SHE'S happy, with a new content
That feels to her like Sacrament.
She's busy, with an altered care,
As just apprenticed to the Air.

She's tearful, if she weep at all,
For blissful causes, — most of all
That Heaven permit so meek as she
To such a Fate to minister.

SHE staked her feathers, gained an arc,
Debated, rose again, —
This time beyond the inference
Of Envy — or of Men.

And now among circumference
Her steady boat be seen —
At ease among the billows
As the bough where she was born.

THE morning after woe,
'Tis frequently the way,
Surpasses all that rose before
For utter jubilee;

As Nature did not care
And piled her blossoms on,
The further to parade a joy
Her victim stared upon.

The birds declaim their tunes,
Pronouncing every word
Like hammers. Did they know they fell
Like Litanies of lead

On here and there a creature,
They'd modify the glee
To fit some Crucifixial clef,
Some key of Calvary!

UNIT, like Death, for whom?
True — like the Tomb
Who tells no secret
Told to him.

The Grave is strict —
Tickets admit
Just two — the Bearer
And the Borne —

And seat just One.
The Living tell
The Dying but a syllable;
The coy Dead — none.

136

IT was a grave, yet bore no stone,
Enclosed 'twas not by rail;
A consciousness its acre,
It held a human soul.

Entombed by whom, for what offense,
If home — or foreign born,
Had I the curiosity
'Twere not appeased of Man.

Till Resurrection I must guess,
Denied the small desire
A rose upon its ridge to sow,
Or palliate a briar.

BETWEEN my Country
  And the Others
There is a Sea —
  But flowers
Negotiate between us
  As ministry.

(In the old grave-yard)

THE color of the grave is green, —
The outer grave, I mean, —
You would not know it from the field
Except it own a stone.

It helps the Fond to find it,
Too infinite asleep
To stop and tell them where it is,
But just a daisy deep.

The color of the grave is white, —
The Winter grave, I mean, —
You would not know it from the drifts
In Winter, till the Sun

Has furrowed out the aisles, —
Then higher than the land
The little dwelling houses rise
Where each has left a Friend.

The color of the grave within, —
The duplicate, I mean, —
Not all the snows could make it white —
Not all the Summers, green.

You've seen the color, maybe,
Upon a bonnet bound,
When that you met it with before,
The ferret cannot find.

A FIRST mute coming
In the stranger's house —
A first fair going
When the bells rejoice —

A first exchange
Of what hath mingled firm
For lot — exhibited
To Faith alone.

PUT up my lute — what of my music!
Since the sole ear I cared to charm
Passive as granite laps my music,
Sobbing will suit as well as psalm!

Would but the Memnon of the desert
Teach me the strain that vanquished him
When he surrendered to the Sunrise —
Maybe that would awaken them!

NO man can compass a despair.
As round a goalless road
No faster than a mile at once
The traveller proceed —
Unconscious that the sun
Be setting on his progress —
So accurate the one
At estimating pain
Whose own has just begun.
His ignorance the Angel
That pilot him along.

GOOD to have had them lost
For news that they are saved!
The nearer they departed us
The nearer they — restored —

Shall stand to our right hand.
Most precious are the Dead, —
Most precious those that turned to go,
Then thought of us — and stayed!

THE province of the Saved
Should be the art to save
Through skill obtained within themselves.
The science of the grave

No man can understand
But he that hath endured
The dissolution in himself;
That man be qualified

To certify Despair
To those who, failing new,
Mistake Defeat for Death each time —
Till acclimated to.

DESPAIR'S advantage is achieved
By suffering, — despair
To be assisted of reverse
One must have previous borne.

The worthiness of suffering,
Like the excellence of Death,
Is ascertained by tasting —
As can no other mouth

Of savours make us conscious,
As did ourselves partake.
Affliction feels impalpable
Until ourselves are struck!

THAT after horror that was Us —
That passed the mouldering pier
Just as the granite crumb let go,
Our savior by a hair —

A second more had dropped too deep
For fisherman to plumb —
The very profile of the thought
Puts recollection numb!

The possibility to pass,
Without a moment's bell,
Into Conjecture's presence —
Is like a face of steel

That suddenly looks into ours
With a metallic grin, —
The cordiality of Death
Who drills his welcome in.

'TIS so appalling it exhilarates!
So over-horror it half captivates!
The Soul stares after it — secure,
To know the worst leaves no dread more.
To scan a ghost is faint,
But grappling conquers it.
How easy torment now —
Suspense kept sawing so!
The truth is bald and cold,
But that will hold.
If any are not sure,
We show them prayer —
But we who know
Stop hoping now.
Looking at Death is Dying —
Just let go the breath,
And not the pillow at your cheek
So slumbereth.
Others can wrestle, yours is done,
And so of woe bleak dreaded, come —
It sets the fright at liberty,
And terror's free —
Gay, ghastly holiday!

THE test of Love is Death,
Our Lord "so loved", it saith;
What Largest Lover hath —
Another doth!

If smaller patience be
Through less infinity,
If bravo sometimes swerve
Through fainter nerve,

Accept its most —
And overlook the dust.
Last, least,
The Cross' request!

A NEARNESS to Tremendousness
An Agony procures,
Affliction ranges Boundlessness.
Vicinity to laws
Contentment's quiet suburb, —
Affliction cannot stay
In acre or location —
It rents Immensity.

ONLY God possess the secret,
Only God!
The Jehovahs are no babblers.
Unto God
God the Son disclose it,
Still secure.
God the Spirit's honor
Equal sure.

APPENDIX

THE Editors are aware that to familiar and instinctive readers of the poems of Emily Dickinson any explanation of her meaning or phrasing would be unwelcome. It has, however, been pointed out that in certain cases the Poet's extraordinary condensation has proved baffling to those less accustomed.

For the benefit of these, as well as for students, the Editors have in the present instance been requested to suggest the words omitted, but which may be understood, in the second stanza of the poem, "More life went out, when He went," on page four.

In Emily Dickinson's own manuscript these lines read: —

The climate of the grave
A temperature just adequate
So anthracite to live.

Amplified, by inclusion in the reader's mind of the words omitted by the Poet, her meaning becomes: —

The climate of the grave (being)
A temperature just adequate
(For One) so anthracite (as He) to live —

"anthracite" in her sense referring to a glowing, combustible substance.

INDEX OF FIRST LINES